Can I Create what Stars Can't Foretell?

Dinesh Sahay

Clever Fox
PUBLISHING
Chennai • Bangalore

CLEVER FOX PUBLISHING
Chennai, India

Published by CLEVER FOX PUBLISHING 2020

ISBN 978-81-946818-1-6

ABOUT DINESH SAHAY

–Author Mentor

An award-winning author who was born in Jhansi, Uttar Pradesh, India, his late father was a mechanical engineer, MIE, and his late grandfather was a Courtier in the Kingdom of King Madhav Rao Scindhiya in Gwalior, Madhya Pradesh, India.

Dinesh Sahay (BSc, CBIM), has worked in many companies as ex. GM, Techno link Engineering Co Pvt Ltd, Techno Trade, Senior Manager Marketing & Sales, Kumar Oxygen Ltd, Kumaun Gases Ltd, DM, Modi Rubber Ltd and other reputed companies. During this period, he guided many of his members, clients, distributors, dealers, and employees of the company about his programme, ***"Enlighten the Lamp of your Fortune"*** which was towards positive creation in life. Many members joined him for this programme during his service period and after. The programme was a great success (for example, businesses, finances, and other sectors).

With the vast practical experience in the **Art of Creation**, he started his **online programme "Make Your Dreams Come True" and *"Enlighten the Lamp of your Fortune"*** in 2003. He interacted with members online through blogs and social media. He distributed his programme book in PDF format. He shared this PDF book through email to all his members who joined him for this programme.

Finally, the story of the author's journey began by writing and publishing one book, **"Enlighten the Lamp of your Fortune" in 2018.** The book was published in 2018 and it was pertaining to wish/dream fulfilment and solutions for individual problems of life. The book received great reviews as i it was a completely new subject which had an actual programme for wish/dream fulfilment. He wrote a series of books thereafter and continues to do so.

He wrote another book, "Miracles Through My Eyes," which was based on the real-life experiences of the people who were connected with the author including himself, and the miracles happened. In everyone's lives **Both the books were a big success, especially among younger people, and those who had problems in life or those who wanted their wishes fulfilled.**

He has written five books, three in English and two in Hindi. Two books are under publishing process (one in English and the other is in Tamil).

He won the best Author Award, a trophy and a certificate for his book, "Miracles Through My Eyes"

at New Town Book Fair 2020 held at Kolkata on 1st January 2020.

The best Author Award, trophy and a certificate was given for the above-mentioned book as under;

1. **Litroma 75 Rising Stars Award 2020.**
2. **Critic Space Online Journal – for Top-100 Debut Novels**

(His book, "Miracles Through My Eyes" was selected as India's one of the Top-100 Debut Novels under the survey of literatureslight & Critic Space Journal. The book was selected based on the reviews and the popularity of the author among the readers.)

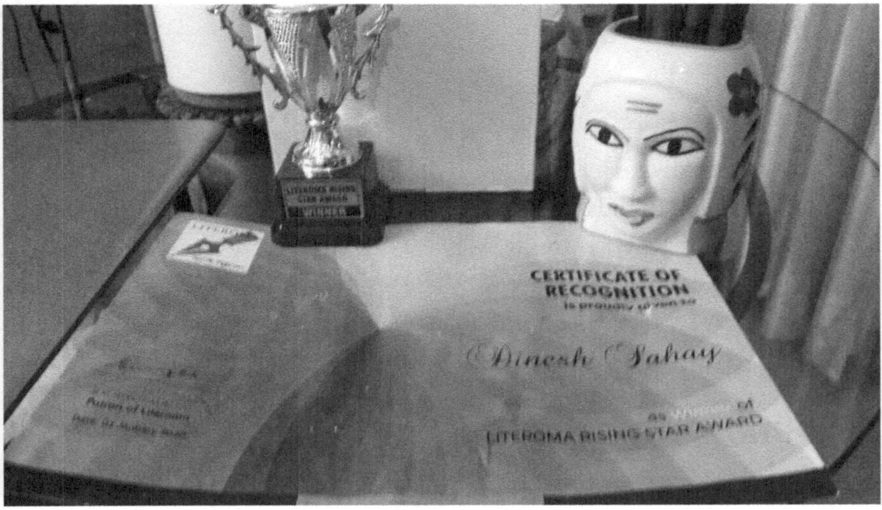

Certificate of Appreciation

TOP 100 DEBUT NOVELS

THIS CERTIFICATE IS PROUDLY PRESENTED TO

Dinesh Sahay

For book "Miracles Through My Eyes", which has been featured as India's one of "Top 100 Debut Novels" under the survey of Literatureslight & Criticspace Literary Journal. We congratulate you for this outstanding achievement and wish you every possible success in your future literary career.

The top 100 debut novels have been selected as per the reviews of book and popularity of author among the readers.

Authorized Signatory
www.literatureslight.com

Date: 30th March 2020

Authorized Signatory
www.criticspace.com

ENGLISH

1. Miracles Through My Eyes
   (Worldwide release)
2. Enlighten the Lamp of your Fortune. (Worldwide release)
3. Art of Staying Young While Growing Old (Worldwide release)
4. Can I Create what Stars Can't Foretell? Current book

HINDI

1. Mastishk aur Vicharo se Jeevan ki Rachna Kaise Kare? (Worldwide release)

2. Vradh Hone par Yuva Rahne ki Kala (Worldwide release) book

3. Tamil: book has been published which is the translation of English book, "Can I Create What Stars Can't Foretell?

Important Note:

There is an important collaboration with an artist Valbhi Garg.

ARTIST-VALBHI GARG Instagram profile @ aesthetic_artistry06 has made **three paintings for this book** and she is collaborating with me for my future projects also.

WEBSITE LINKS

https://authordineshsahaybooks.blogspot.com/

https://www.authordineshsahay.in/

http://dineshsahaybook.com/

AUTHOR EMAIL

query.makeyourdreams@gmail.com; enlightenthelamp@gmail.com

DEDICATION

I dedicate this book to my late Grandfather, Mother & Father. I am presenting this book to the readers and sharing my views which I learned under their guidance. Without their blessings I would not have been an author.

Dinesh Sahay

9 July 2020

My late Grandfather

Late Mother & Father & sister & myself

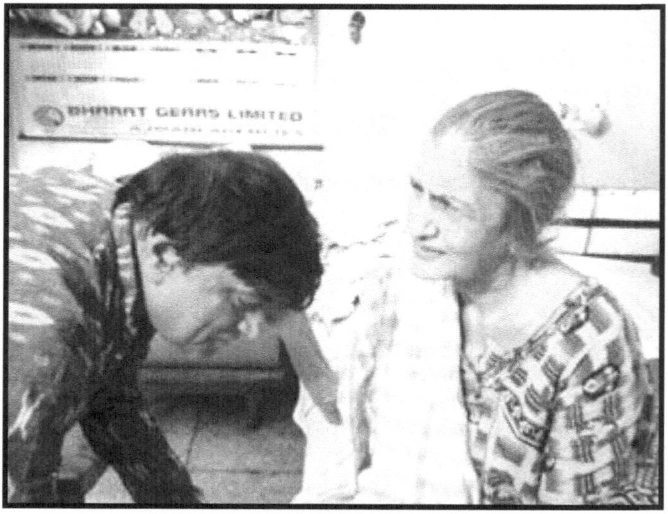

Taking blessing with my Mother

CONTENTS

PREFACE

This book is a guide to find solutions to problems faced by people in their lives such as financial, business, job, health, and personal problems. There can be many such issues. The cause and effect theory plays its role for all the problems in life which are self-created and the solution lies with self-analysis and correction. If there is a problem, there is a solution. The book contains a practical approach in the form of a lesson where one can read and start a programme for wish fulfilment. One can set a goal or a wish in actual life and set a target date as per choice. How can one build millionaire consciousness? How one can create life and destiny with least efforts and become rich and abundant? How to create what you want in actual life? This book will give you some positive sense as to why some people fail in their lives but others are very successful.

How can you change your pre-set notions, stop riding on negative aspects of life, and bring 360 degrees change to transform your life as per choice with set targets and date? When you read this book and follow the programmes on your own, you will observe a change in your thinking, speaking, and actions on ground.

Dinesh Sahay
Author & Mentor
9 July 2020

INTRODUCTION

I wish to share information about my initial programme of wish/dream fulfilment and solutions to problems of life, ***"Enlighten the Lamp of your Fortune"*** which I was conducting previously, I had provided a PDF format book to my members and wished to write a book on this subject and selected the tittle of the book as, ***"Can I Create What Stars Can't Foretell?***

Now it is possible, so I am presenting my readers with this book about the ethics of creation of life events. Once you know the art of creation of events in actual life, then you can become master and can wish what you want in life. God is ever ready to fulfil your demands subject to universal rules of nature/God.

I hope it will be an interesting read. Thanks.

Dinesh Sahay
Author-Mentor
Date 9 July 2020
Email: query.makeyourdreams@gmail.com
enlightenthelamp@gmail.com

CHAPTER 1

BEGIN JOURNEY WITH UNIVERSAL RULES OF NATURE/GOD

There are some unimaginable thoughts which must be pricking in your mind and you want to explore the answers of such questions throughout your life. Here are some of them;

Is the life we lead really destined for us?

Has God written our destiny before we were born into this world?

Is our destiny determined by our actions in previous births?

Can we become what we want in our lives?

Can we live till when we want to live?

Can we become rich with the little we have at present?

Can we cure ourselves and recover from diseases?

Can we find a life partner destined for us in this life?

Can we marry a person of our choice by God's grace?

Can any person living in a hut dream about a palace and become very rich?

Can people with special needs lead a happy and successful life?

Can we create our life as per our wishes, dreams, and goals?

My answer to all the above questions is big yes!

We can cure ourselves and recover from diseases.

You can find a life partner destined for you in this life. You can marry a person of your choice by God's grace.

A person living in a hut can dream about a palace and become very rich.

People with special needs can lead a happy and successful life.

We can create anything at any point of time!

You can do whatever you wish/dream, but will have to make a 360 degree change in your nature and mind-set, erase old negative notions, and add some good actions into your life.

About the programme, Enlighten the Lamp of your Fortune*

In this programme, you can easily create your life as per your set goal/dream/wish, by God's grace, subject to laws of the nature. I have designed it using the technique of power of thought, power of spoken word, power of mind, and power of writing.

The method of this programme is given in different chapters of this book.

Let's first understand how we create our lifecycle and destiny, before we start this programme. Many people have spoken differently about fate and was described in many religious books by avatars like Lord Rama, Sri Krishna, Jesus Christ, and many other ancient sages.

Different religions and faiths have their own reasoning but in **Santana Dharma, ancient Sage Yogi Vashishtha had described fate as:**

"Fate or destiny/Kismet is the invention of fools and does not exist. Whoever believes in it and is obsessed with divine fate, is the enemy of his own soul. He perishes, destroying his own good worth and prosperity." (Yogi Vashishtha)

You are the creator of your own destiny stored for you by God. He releases it to you on demand by your thoughts and actions. It is as simple as this.

Your destiny is locked between your past and present thoughts. It is a fight between past thoughts and the present ones. The thoughts that strive hard, win.

Thoughts are manifested in life accordingly, successfully or unsuccessfully. In the materialistic world, nothing is impossible.

Every thought is taking shape and vibrates to the impression of time, space, matter, and action. The one who strives harder, wins. Self-effort and self-analysis are the road to success. This requires knowledge (gyana) and action (karma). The application of discipline, analysis, wise company, and good actions are the parameters of the formation of a good future…it is simple and that's it."

Yogi Vashishtha

You lead your life in the present moment of your time, whether it's life or death. Forget about the past, which is gone. Ignore it and look forward to the creation of your destiny in the present moments of your life. Future is undefined and you have to create it. Your spoken words are the door to your destiny which you create…it is simple and that's it.

Your intent becomes your thought which opens up the pathway to destiny…it is simple and that's it. Your thoughts manifest and become your destiny…it is simple and that's it.

Your actions open up your direction to destiny…it is simple and that's it.

You create destiny deep inside your inner self and see the reflection and manifestation of it on the outer platform of the world, in the spiritual and materialistic form in life. **Richness/abundance is a possibility with least efforts…it is simple and that's it.**

Giving is receiving, means; what you give that comes back to you, whether it is love or hate, money, truth, blessings, appreciation, thankfulness, contentment, and gratitude…it is simple and that's it.

Happiness is a state of mind which cannot come through wealth but comes by serving mankind…it is simple and that's it.

All forms of diseases are the creation of human behavior by virtue of negative thoughts and a negative action (karma) of self and others…it is simple and that's it.

Hate, violence, quarrels, and anger keep abundance, money, and wealth away…it is simple and that's it.

You attract what you love, may it be money, or anything…it is simple and that's it. Love unites all and creates a pathway for building your destiny…it is simple and that's it.

You lose what you hate and violate the set rules of nature (love, affection, sharing), let it be friend, wife, husband, money, or wealth, no matter what it is and whoever he/she may be…it is simple and that's it.

All bad events come into your lives because of the negative factors, which you should know.

You lose money and wealth if you use them for personal and selfish means and do not share it with the needy and poor...it is simple and that's it.

Avoid speaking about death and suicide about self and others which may cause this event in the life of a person including self, as life and death stays in the power of tongue...it is simple and that's it.

Gossiping and talking bad about anyone can wreck lives. Avoid this.

If you are facing failures or bad events in your life, remember you had created it all for yourself, just analyze your past mistakes and improve and look forward strongly in a positive way. People around you are the helpers sent by God in the creation of your destiny. Love them, wish them, help them, give, and share what they want with what you have. You will create good events in your life by God's will and grace.

Use money and wealth for the benefit of others, keep it in circulation and use it and share it with others too, otherwise it will go away from you in many ways. **You cannot keep money in fixed deposits, lockers, shares, and in the form of property. If kept with selfish motive and not utilized for charity for the needy and poor and those who have sought help in difficult times, it will be taken back by God in many other ways (diseases, illness, thefts, fire, robbery). It is the natural law of**

sharing which one must follow. Remember God is ever ready to work with you in every need if it is without any selfish motive but will not prefer to work only for you alone.

How life actually works for a man?

Remember that your mind is like a tape/video recorder and all which you see, listen, and speak is recorded constantly in recorder or conscious mind. Now your subconscious mind sends signals to God. He (God) later observes and selects some of the impressions from it, and then He replays it for you in your life as you previously have recorded it. Thus, our five senses of the body play a major role and are responsible for all creation in terms of events happening and situations in life.

What is happening within our inner-selves is basically the reflections, which actually are coming out on the outer platform of the world through our Sub-Conscious Mind either in the form of worldly or spiritual means in our lives. God has given us the option to lead life as per our choice, but we forget what He (God) likes and what He doesn't like. He, however, wants us to lead our life in a way where one will have to explore deep inside our mental consciousness by performing meditation for search of "who am I?" He also wants us to follow the set rules of Nature/Universe/God, whatever you believe in.

People live longer because they have long goals with long targets in life or they continuously make multi-goals and target them for different periods and when one ends another begins. But some people live shorter because they have set short goals and when they accomplish it, their purpose of life ends, and they depart, and end the journey of life.

People who are dissatisfied or unhappy with their life normally end their lives too early. People who live in the future, plan in it sometimes don't live to see their plans.

Fear of anything leads to misfortune, for example, fear of drowning, accident, and death. The best way is to set a goal/wish/dream, and then plan it in the present and have a vision for the future, only then you may reach somewhere near to your goals or manifest your dreams.

There are some important suggestions to lead a positive life

To lead a positive life, one has to develop good habits and leave bad habits simultaneously. One must lead life as God and nature want us to lead. Please practice them in your lives.

Love is a real tool of creation and its opposite hate is a negative tool of destruction.

1. Love anyone or anything you want in life; it will attract the same. Love unites all, it does all creation, expands, and manifests before you in life. It can be anybody or anything, in this materialistic world.

2. **Trust yourself and others,** if you are in the company of nice people around you. Trust that you are an all-powerful child of God and you shall be successful in whatever you do in life, even if you have failed initially.

   All successful men were unsuccessful in the beginning of their initial attempts in lives but became famous thereafter.

3. **FAITH in GOD and FAITH in SELF** that you can do anything, with blessing of your Guru, teacher, and mentor. It is important for your life as a whole. If you don't believe in self and don't love yourself, then how can you love God? So, love yourself as you are, love everyone as they may be. Then you will love and believe in God.

4. **POWER OF SHARING** (share what you have with others, especially the poor, downtrodden, underprivileged, disabled, whether it be in terms of money, wealth, service, help, education etc.). Charity is the biggest investment, so contribute some percentage of your income every month (if in service) or annually (if you are in business or a corporate) for charity. If you contribute 10% of your income regularly you will have Millionaire Consciousness and shall get huge successes as far as position or wealth is concerned through infinite intelligence.

5. **POWER OF GIVING,** because giving is receiving, it is a natural law. **Giving is a natural law** because when you start to give others, then you start receiving

pleasantries from the Universe. God is pleased and rewards you.

6. **POWER OF TONGUE, YOUR SPOKEN WORDS,** MANTRAS, MELODIOUS SOUND from the mouth or through an instrument have power to create good for all. It is an important tool in the creation of all events, good or bad in your life accordingly as you speak. **Think twice what you speak and speak what you want in your life and what you don't want.**
7. **LIVE SIMPLE but have high thoughts for the wellbeing of others.**
8. **BELIEVE AND THINK BIG.** Whenever you are thinking, keep your thoughts very big and in high esteem. There may be impossible targets, but you will see they can be achieved later.
9. **HAVE LONG TIME-BOUND TARGETED GOALS AND BREAK IT in SUB-GOALS.** You will reach nowhere if you do not have a dream, goal, or wish in your life.
10. **TALK TO SELF** what you want, it will reach God; Write it daily.
11. **REVIEW YOUR WISH/DREAM/GOAL EVERY DAY WITHOUT FAIL**
12. You are the creator of all your problems and also solutions to all your problems; others are only subjects or objects. What happened in your life was due to cause and effect theory. God is simply creating

what you ask, think, act and whatever you do, it comes back to you exactly as you created it.

13. Your time is eternal so don't wait and procrastinate. Don't say "I am busy", instead say "My time is eternal and I can manage all in my life efficiently as per deadline." If not in this lifecycle, then in the other births also. You are a winner both ways.

14. Respect and love all including your enemies.

15. Avoid anger, hatred, gossip, jealousy, talking bad about people, and greed as they are all negative tools of negative creation of events in life.

16. Avoid all doubts, fears, mistrust, violence, anger, negative talks, and thoughts as they are all negative tools which are responsible for all negative events and happenings in life.

CHAPTER 2

HOW TO ERASE NEGATIVITY & PAST NEGATIVE RECORDS FROM MIND?

In this chapter, you can see the method of the programme, "Enlighten the Lamp of your Fortune*" and also review tips about succeeding through this programme. Review tips related to removing negative thoughts, preparing wish slips, holding your thoughts, and taking precautions.

Affirmations

Read these affirmations in the morning and several times before you start reading your wish slip.

Take an A4 size paper. Fold it twice and cut into four pieces or fold thrice and cut into eight pieces for writing your wish, dream, or goal. Take a pencil and eraser or pen and write your wish in a precise manner, with the date by which you want to see your wish to manifest.

"I confess all my sins, may all such sins be erased from my mind and go back to nothingness. My soul is now purified."

"I empty my mind from all doubts, foolishness, stupidity, and ineptness. I now fill my mind with God's truth and see it coming and taking possession of all my problems since I believe in the God, I will get the results, the right answer will come."

"By my spoken words, I smash and demolish every untrue record from my subconscious mind. It came from the dust heap of the native nothingness for they came from my own vain happenings. I now make my perfect records through God within, the records of health wealth, love, and perfect self-expression."

"Divine love dissolves and dissipates every wrong condition from my mind, body, and affairs. Divine love is the most powerful chemical of the universe which dissolves everything which is not of itself."

Wish Slips

Write your wish on a slip of paper. If you are doing this for the first time, keep a copy of it in your Dream Box.

Here are some tips for creating wish slips:

Take time to write and correct your wish slip in present tense until you find that it satisfies your conscious mind and no negative questions come to your mind. You can change the wish or update it any day. Sometimes, the date by which you wanted to achieve your wish is crossed. Extend the date, because you have fixed the wrong date which your mind had never accepted.

If you want to continue with what you have originally written, then be positive and think that God and the Universe, which is unlimited will create for you what you demanded, since God has no limitations. Write a fresh wish slip every morning with a date and a spiritual symbol on it as per your religion, few minutes before you read. Then place old slip in Dream Box or you can destroy it. If you keep in the Dream Box, then you can assess the results after your wish is manifested. Continue the process till you reach near to your goal/dream or wish is manifested. See the procedure further in the chapter.

Do not write any wish against anyone or to harm anyone. This is clearly stated in the terms and conditions. By doing so you are doing harm to the person and at the same time you will receive similar negative actions in your life. Make good wishes for yourself, your family, company, and business to benefit others.

Observe that when you write your wish, many negative questions can come to your mind. How can I become CEO, when I am not even qualified for the same? How can I get this fat salary?

Holding Your Thoughts

Each day, write your wish on the wish slip. Read it and say it aloud during each time zone of the day. Destroy this wish slip the next day after you write a fresh wish slip.

On the first day of the programme, write your wish on two wish slips. On the first **wish slip,** write the date when the programme started and keep it in the **Dream Box. The Dream Box** is not to be opened till your wish is manifested. Keep the other wish slip with you for the whole day to read and destroy it the next morning after you write a fresh wish slip for the day. When one goal/ dream is manifested, start another similarly.

Read the wish slip exactly in each time zone – 6 am, 12 noon, 6 pm, 12 am midnight (or when you go to sleep). During these times, thoughts are transferred from conscious mind to subconscious mind. **The period of thought transfer is short – a few seconds to a minute. Read your wish slip quickly and constantly in a low voice audible only to you. Ensure that your watch is accurate. Start reading from 5.58 am to 6.02 am so that your thoughts may transfer exactly at 6 am and likewise for the other time.**

Remember the following points:

Observe the daily activity to identify the happenings in the direction of your wish/dream. All creation in your life will start the moment the thought is transferred to the subconscious mind, which may take less or more time, but rest assured something will definitely manifest in a few days.

Act on the responses such as, a telephone call coming from unexpected or known sources, some news in newspaper, email, anyone visiting you and giving information, or any unexpected activity or event, which is in the direction of your dream/wish.

Act upon them even if they do not completely match your wish, because you never know what is coming next. Accepting and acting on the first observation does not mean that you forego or give up your original wish. Keep reading the wish slips till you achieve the ultimate results.

How life actually works for a man?

There is nothing like destiny in a man's life which many people believe and depend on this concept. Life is your own creation which you knowingly or unknowingly create within you. You have to seek for it within yourself, think about it, plan and execute as per fixed deadline. **If you go to a Temple what you will find there? A statue of God either blessing you with the pose of one hand towards you "Giving a blessing" or pose with one hand down like in a famous Shri Tirupati Balaji Temple or any Temple you go worldwide. The meaning behind this example, I want to say that even God gives you want you to ask from Him, and without His blessing, nothing is blessed. Blessings are given when you are qualified for such good practices such as Laws of the Universe, God, or Nature.**

You have to choose what type of life you wish to perform. There are three ways for you to choose from; 1. A spiritual way of life, or 2. Worldly life and 3. Leave it to God and let it come as He does. In the first case,

usually the people enter in this spiritual life only after they achieve some wishes in their lives then proceed further. In second case almost everyone follows this, because it's a life in which Karm (duties) are considered to be of necessary and important for everyone. Lord Shri Krishan in Gita has explained Arjuna about the Karma and it is also a path to salvation. Lastly, third way will depend on your paste Karmas of previous birth cycle which will play its role in creating your destiny, but it could be changed by wise thinking and actions in the present life.

In all the three options I would recommend readers to do self-introspection and analysis within yourself and work then choose and follow that in your lives.

CHAPTER 3

HOW CAN YOU LEAD LIFE AS PER YOUR DREAMS?

Let's refresh what you have read in previous chapter, before starting the procedure for this programme, remember:

There are three levels of the Mind: Conscious; Subconscious; and Unconscious. Conscious and Subconscious mind play a role in the creation of destiny. Subconscious mind is like God's mind, which receives signals from conscious mind and does all creation in life in the form of events and happenings.

Thoughts are formed in our conscious state of mind through the five senses, eyes, ears, touch, smell, taste inside and outside of this body, the world, and even the universe. Thoughts are formed as we see through our eyes, upon hearing and what we speak about others and what is around us. Concentrate on those that can contribute something good in our lives.

Time consists of three stages, past, present, and future and destiny is created as per our thoughts in the past, present, and future. What we see today is due to our past thoughts and actions. We create our life depending on the quality of our thoughts. Create your thoughts by writing your wish or a goal or dream on paper. You cannot write without thinking. It is the writing process that ensures the formation of your thought in perfect way.

There are four-time zones. Feed these thoughts into your subconscious mind in each time zone systematically by speaking to yourself. Thoughts are thus fed into the mind from the conscious level to the subconscious level step by step. The subconscious mind receives these impressions and sends it to God/Universe/ Nature (whatever you believe) for manifestation.

Hold your thoughts by your vocal cord and speech, since thoughts come and go and disappear from the conscious mind very fast. Speak to yourself constantly for a few minutes to hold the thoughts, so that the subconscious mind can carry some of its impressions.

Be very positive when you start the programme and believe that your wish is going to be manifested. It is a thought transfer from conscious to subconscious mind and it is just a matter of time. It can take from one day to the date you choose. This will depend on factors around you, such as people, friends, family, situations, and your mindset – positive or negative – about this programme.

All creations are manifested by God. We only demand and He commands everything that exists in the universe.

G-O-D is the Generator–Organizer–Deliverer. All people connected with us in the present life are helpers sent by Him. If we ignore, fight, harm, or annoy them, this is when we face problems or difficulties and don't get what we want. Follow the set rules of nature – love, sharing, helping, gratitude, appreciation, and thankfulness – to maintain good relations with all.

CHAPTER 4

WHAT ARE TIME ZONES IN 24 HOURS OF THE DAY?

There are four time zones in each day. The Earth rotates in the orbit of sun, which decides the time and positions of the day on our planet Earth. The four positions of the day are morning, afternoon, evening, and night. The sun and its satellites in the solar system, Earth, Jupiter, Venus, Mars, Uranus, Mercury, Neptune, Pluto, and Saturn, are the part of the Universe which are connected to Divine Intelligence.

These time zones are very important in our lives not only because our life's working revolves around them, but also due to their effect on thoughts and spoken words on the conscious and the subconscious mind. Especially, it affects our mind at 6 am when the night meets the morning, 12 noon when morning meets the afternoon, 6 pm when afternoon meets the evening, and 12 am when evening meets the night. Now it is very important for you to note that these time zones are important because during this period, thoughts are transferred usually from conscious to subconscious mind. Therefore, I have used these timings in the programme as all creation and manifestation of events and happenings are done by this technique of the Miraculous Power of Mind in my programme, "Enlighten the lamp of your fortune*" for wish/dream/goal fulfilment.

You must have heard from your parents or grandparents or older adults that one should not speak bad words when it is morning or evening or when you go to sleep. The experienced people have seen its effect on their life's journey that events are manifested accordingly in their lives, as the thought, spoken words do affect the life creation during these time zones.

CHAPTER 5

HOW DOES THE PROGRAMME, "ENLIGHTEN THE LAMP OF YOUR FORTUNE" WORK?

This programme, "Enlighten the Lamp of your Fortune*" is very simple, where you can create your life as per your set goal/dream/wish. I have designed it using the technique of power of thought, power of spoken word, power of mind, and power of writing. All creation comes from our thoughts, spoken words, and actions through Miraculous Power of Mind. The mind is a powerful part or tool of the body which controls the inner and outer body, and all activities of an individual on the outer platform of the world through Divine Intelligence.

There are three levels of mind: first is **conscious mind**; second is **subconscious mind;** and third is **unconscious mind**. Conscious mind is when we are in a conscious state and aware about what is happening around us. Unconscious is when we are in sleep or not active mentally.

Subconscious mind is God's mind. It does all creations in our life as per impressions of our thoughts and spoken words.

Thoughts are continuously created in our mind by virtue of our five senses, inner feelings of the body and mind, and through what is around us.

Our belief systems, feelings (good or bad), preset notions, habits, intent, they all create thoughts and create events and happenings in our lives through the impressions of the subconscious mind. So, thoughts become things in our life.

In fact, you create what you believe or think or speak with complete faith and trust. You go to the Temple/Church/Mosque/Gurudwara and pray and seek God's blessings for your wish/dream/goal and with complete trust and faith in God, you get all. The statue or place of God or Temple/Church/Mosque is just a symbol.

You create everything within you. What you see outside is the reflection in the form of materialistic or spiritual world. You are not going to get anything good in your life if you have doubts, negative belief system, negative thoughts and feelings, preset notions, and negative speech.

THREE STATES OF MIND

(Conscious) **(Sub-Conscious)** **(Unconscious)**

When you are not in conscious state of mind & in deep sleep)

(It's a Godly mind which receives selected thoughts, words, feeling through five senses from conscious-mind, and it manifests event, happenings and creation in life).

(Thoughts are manufactured in the conscious mind through our belief systems, preset notions, behavior, intent, feelings, and habits. Such thoughts carry from previous births and from our present life. It is a continuous process where one is in a conscious state of mind and frequent thoughts keep hovering in the mind (except when one is in complete command and control in thoughtless meditation). Thoughts are manufactured through the five senses of the body, the five senses can be described in a simple word, as sensory details the body receives from the eyes, nose, ears, tongue, and inner and outer body).

------------ Good/positive ---------

Good thoughts and actions done for the benefit of others, such as love, thankfulness, kindness, gratitude, appreciation, help, charity, compassion, respect, and sympathy.

---------------Bad/negative---------------

Bad/negative thoughts and actions are responsible for the creation of bad events in one's life, such as, anger, jealousy, quarrels, envy, torture, violence, harassment, fights, and gossip.

What happens when a particular thought enters the conscious mind?

When any strong thought enters the conscious mind, it remains in it for some time. Then your subconscious mind takes impressions of the received good or bad thoughts from the conscious mind and the subconscious mind does all creation in your life which is a part of God's mind.

Destiny

This becomes your destiny, happenings, and events in your future life.

Creation of events is due to your past thoughts, spoken words, and action in this life and what you carry through previous births. We can win over the past and create good fortune in the present.

Here in my programme, "Enlighten the Lamp of Your Fortune", you transfer your thoughts in the form of wish/dream/goal to the subconscious mind, which sends signals for creation to God, the Universe, Nature who do all the creation as events and happenings in your life.

All depends on how a single strong thought is transferred from conscious to subconscious mind, with complete trust, faith, and belief. Once the thought is transferred, the manifestation is bound to come from God's will. Whenever or whatever you ask God, He says, Tathastu! (meaning May it happens for you as you desire).

It is only a matter of time to transfer the thought which may be in hours/days/months. Thought transfer will depend on some negative factors, which should be kept in check and controlled by you during the programme so that the programme goes smoothly. Some positive factors like faith, trust, and belief make this process faster, but negative ones like doubts, suspicions, and negative talking may reverse the process.

CHAPTER 6

WHAT ARE THE ITEMS FOR USE IN THE PROGRAMME?

"Enlighten the Lamp of Your Fortune*" programme is 100% successful and well tested. So, you have to start this with lot of faith, trust, and belief that you are sure to see your dreams come true.

Follow the procedure as given in this book. You should keep ready the following items, known as tools for this programme, until such time that you are doing this programme.

1. A-4 size paper, 12 to 15 in number. Please fold the paper twice to make 4 slips or thrice to make 8 slips. Use these as wish slips for the programme.
2. One carton box, small in size, 1ft long × 4/5 inches in width, or any small box with a hole where written wish is kept inside without opening the box. Please paste a slip and name the box as Wish Box or Dream Box. Please ensure that the box is sealed properly

and should not be opened till you are doing this programme. It can be opened when you feel that you have successfully achieved what you have wished. You can add your wish one by one in the Dream Box.

3. Please keep an alarm clock ready for the programme and ensure that it's time is accurate. Time is a very important factor and you have to follow it with utmost accuracy.

4. A pencil, sharpener, rubber or eraser, and a pen are important tools in this programme.

CHAPTER 7

WHAT ARE THE PRECAUTIONS TO FOLLOW BEFORE AND DURING THE PROGRAMME?

You have to take many precautions during and before the start of this programme. Since it is a mental and spiritual programme, any negativity or bad action from your side will hamper the ultimate result. You should have complete faith and trust while you do this programme as it is already tested on many and the success rate is fantastic.

Some of the important precautions are as follows:

1. Be calm/comfortable, relaxed, and quiet. If you have time, sit for 5 to 6 minutes in silence. Watch your breath going in and out, meditate and relax.
2. Speak when it is necessary otherwise remain silent and think about your dream. Think as if it has

already been accomplished and what you would do thereafter. For example, if you want a car, imagine that you are driving the car with your family. It is a visualization technique.

3. **The mind has unlimited potential and knowledge which creates everything of your choice.** But we limit our mind with the present resources at our disposal. Sky has unlimited space. Similarly, mind has unlimited abundance and the resources within us are unlimited. **Please remember that everything is achievable if your mind accepts it.** You have to think and believe that, yes, you can do it, you can achieve, you can be rich, you are healthy, you are slim, you are beautiful, you can become what you want, then nothing can stop you from achieving your goal.

4. **When you are doing this programme have no doubts about how it will work out** when you do not have resources at hand for that particular wish/dream. Please remember, the creation comes from Divine Intelligence, God (the Universe), which is unlimited and your present resources do not matter for dream fulfilment.

5. **You will not discuss anything about this programme with anyone** regarding what you are doing and why are you doing it. The simple logic is that the same person with whom you discuss may speak negatively, which may induce negativity on your thoughts and spoil your programme. You

have to maintain absolute secrecy while you do this programme.

6. When you have to write or read during the programme, you have to maintain the strict time schedule as per programme time zones, because at this time your thoughts are transferred from conscious to subconscious mind.

7. **Please avoid** speaking words in daily conversation, like **no, not, don't, can't and all negative talking during the programme.** Your spoken words should be affirmative and positive whenever you talk to anyone during the programme.

8. Please avoid anger, discussions, quarrels, gossip, and jealousy when you are doing this programme. Instead use love, thankfulness, joy, happiness, and appreciation as your tools for life. Any negativity/ anger may affect your programme to some extent.

9. This programme is strictly used to make your good dreams/wishes to come true**. It should not be used for any bad purpose or to harm anyone** as it acts very fast. If used with ulterior motives or with bad intensions, it can harm you. What you send to others, it comes back to you, please remember this.

You have to be absolutely confident and have complete trust in you, God, and this programme, before you start. Remain confident about its success during the programme, "**Enlighten the Lamp of Your Fortune*".** You should never doubt or test this programme at any stage, during or before start of this programme.

You should not think as to how it will make your dreams come true, even if you don't have resources at hand. It has shown remarkable results to me and many others who did this and will definitely surprise you when you start this exercise.

As you proceed with the programme you will observe within three days after the start of the programme, some actions, activities, or event coming in your way in a positive manner which relates to the dream/wish/goal chosen by you. As you feed thought into your brain, action is inevitable and it will come in the form of event or activity by people around you or through a thing, message/phone call/SMS/payment/letter/announcement etc. towards your dream/wish. God sends back to you such events or activities as you feed in your subconscious mind, but success will depend on your actions on the ground.

You have to ensure that you act upon these activities or events which come your way to make your dreams come true. Any inaction from your side is going to affect the programme.

Action is required to achieve success. God will create events for you and you have to accept them by doing action on ground. Any lethargy and procrastination will affect your dream. So, act on it fast. It is a door and pathway to your dream.

CHAPTER 8

SET YOUR GOAL AND BRING CHANGE IN YOUR LIFE

The three stages of time are past, present, and future. The past is dead, the future is unknown, and the present is the time you have. So, set your goal, wish, and dream in present tense when you write it.

Sit at ease and ask what you want in your life – socially, financially, personally, family-wise, career-wise, position-wise, and health-wise. Where do you see yourself in five, ten, fifteen, or thirty years from now? If you have a specific wish or problem, write it in the present tense.

You can divide your goal into sub goals. Do this programme by selecting one goal at a time or all three goals simultaneously. If you concentrate on one goal at a time, it will work faster.

Your wish has to be very specific. Suppose you want a car. This wish is not specific, since it will create questions in your conscious mind. What make? Which colour? New one or used car? Which model? Your subconscious mind will be confused and so will God. Your dream may not manifest the way you want it to. So, write it precisely and be specific with timing. You can write, "I want a brand-new white colored Tata Nano AC car by 2021-06-30."

As you write, many questions come to your mind. How can I get this so soon? So, set your date accordingly, to satisfy your mind. If you want a Mercedes, you may have the thought that there is not enough money for it. Here, you have two options. First, bear in mind that all comes from Divine space, which is unlimited. Second, change your wish to that which satisfies your mind. In any case you have to satisfy your mind in a positive way while you write your final wish or goal.

Write your wish in present tense on pieces of paper – wish slips – and keep tearing them till you arrive at a wish that is complete in all aspects. You should feel that your wish is achievable in the time limit and have no negative questions in mind. In this way, you can create your dreams. The subconscious mind creates for you through God, Divine Intelligence, and Universe. All is possible through the power of mind and spoken words. Be specific, positive, time bound, and without selfish motives. Do not aim to harm anyone or use this against anybody.

CHAPTER 9

GOOD ACTIONS, CHARITY, AND SERVICE TO MANKIND MAKE YOU SUCCESSFUL

You increase the potential of your mind to think big and culminate big and favorable events in your life when you do charity for the poor and needy. It is well tested that contributing 10% of your monthly income or 10% of the earnings annually (if in business or a company) to a charity or for a charitable cause gives you a Millionaire Consciousness.

Those companies or business houses who regularly do charities, make trusts for this purpose, or open hospitals or educational institutions grow faster. No company can grow without it and whichever company works with selfish motives faces problems such as employee's problems, strikes, fires, losses, and lockouts.

However, one can start charity with a small percentage of one's earnings on a regular basis without thinking of its returns. Increase it gradually. This will definitely give you a sense of relief that you are helping humanity.

Any good action by you is returned by the God/ Universe in a way which is always miraculous and unbelievable. Please remember that God is always pleased with any good action from your side and rewards you later, but don't expect this when you do a bad action in your life for anybody.

My programme is partly related to this. I seek support from my readers who do this programme. A part of your earnings from your contribution will be diverted to charitable causes.

CHAPTER 10

WHAT IS THE ACTUAL PROCEDURE OF THE PROGRAMME, "ENLIGHTEN THE LAMP OF YOUR FORTUNE"?

Aladdin's Lamp

There is a story behind my programme, "Enlighten the Lamp of your Fortune", which I want to explain to the readers. You have seen the animated film **Aladdin rubbing a lamp and a Genie appears before him. The Genie says, "Your wish is my command. Tell me your three wishes." Aladdin replies accordingly and the Genie manifests them. My programme is exactly like the Aladdin's magic lamp!**

In this programme, you imagine your **Conscious Mind as a Lamp a**nd play with it. **The Genie is your Subconscious Mind,** which will manifest all that you demand from it. You can demand three wishes at a time. The best way – be precise, ask for one wish at a time, get it, and then go for the others.

Method

Erase all bad and negative thoughts from your mind. You can use the affirmations provided in chapter "Wishes and affirmation" to erase negative thoughts for few days or a week before you start the actual programme.

Set your goal or wish or dream, as provided in the previous chapter on how to do this.

Prepare wish slips. Form your thoughts through writing in wish slips. Follow the method provided in chapters "Important Tools and Equipment" and "What is the procedure…Tips to Success" to prepare your wish slips.

Hold your thought in your conscious mind till it goes to your subconscious mind for few minutes. Do this with your spoken words, so read the wish slip for 2 to 3 minutes slowly so that you can hear your own voice and do it during the time zones at 6 am, 12 pm, 6 pm, and 12 am or while you go to sleep. You can read the details on how to do this in chapter "What is the Procedure"

Follow all the precautions required for the programme in the chapter which provides the details about these precautions. Read the chapter details how you should think during this programme.

Take prompt action on the events and responses that will manifest in the direction of your dream, wish, or goal. If you do not act on responses, it will take considerable time to get the results that you hope for.

Demonstrate your commitment even before your wish is materialized. Start action as if you have achieved the objective. Do something in the direction of your dreams, as if you have already achieved it.

Offer thanks to God when you achieve your objective.

Once you have achieved your objective, do charity for the poor and the needy, or give some part of your earnings to a charitable trust, It could be a simple act. Charity gives you a sense of relief that you are sharing your success with others. At the same time, you please God. You follow the set rules of nature by receiving what you wanted without selfish intentions. It will be good for success and creation in life.

CHAPTER 11

WHAT SHOULD YOU VISUALIZE, SPEAK, FEEL, AND THINK DURING THE PROGRAMME?

Visualization technique will act as a catalyst in making your dreams come true. Follow this daily when you are free. Close your eyes and imagine – if your wish is to have a car – that you are driving the exact car of your dreams with your family. Visualize your house, if that is your wish, and picture yourself in your living room, bedroom, and kitchen.

If your wish is to become a manager or CEO or whatever else, think how you will start your day, how your driver will drive you to work in your big car, how he will hold the car door open for you as you arrive at your office, how you will enter the office, and how everyone will greet you as you move towards your chamber.

If your wish is to work at a particular place, find its address, visit the building, and see it from a distance. You can even walk up to the reception and slowly repeat to yourself, "Look, this is the place where I will work in the near future."

The simple thing is to create a thought which becomes a possibility. At some stage, it will start taking shape in the form of an event that will take you in the direction of the realization of this dream. It may take time, but if you repeat this activity frequently, the results will be faster. You can use this technique if you want faster results, but it is not necessary.

If you want money urgently, say Rs.50,000 or more, write a cheque in your name and sign it from God. Write below "from the bank of the Universe" with the amount. Keep it in your purse or wallet. See it every morning, when you go to sleep and thank God daily for the amount you have received. You will get this amount in your life in due course of time.

There are many ways like this to impress your subconscious mind but follow the method of wish slips which is the perfect way to get what you want. You will reach near to your goals, subject to precautions mentioned earlier, which will be the key factor in making your dreams come true.

CHAPTER 12

HOW TO ACT AND DEMONSTRATE FULFILMENT OF YOUR DREAM/WISH/GOAL?

When you go to a Temple or a Church or a Mosque, you pray to God, "If my wish is achieved, I will distribute sweets to the poor or give charity." If God fulfils it exactly as you demanded, you do what you say to please God and demonstrate your happiness by such action. Similarly, when you do this programme and get what you want, you should demonstrate by such actions of doing charity or distributing something to the poor, to make your dreams a good and lasting success.

Remember that your good actions will please God and your subconscious mind; better will come in your life as you do well to others. I am doing a part of charity on your behalf through the collections, so that you carry the blessings of the people who get it and wish you always for your peace, good health, happiness, and success in life.

May God bless you and make you happy, healthy, and prosperous and I wish that all your dreams may be manifested as you desire in life. Thank you for reading this book.

CHAPTER 13

SELECT AUTO-SUGGESTIONS, AFFIRMATIONS, AND PRAYERS FOR PROGRAMME

You may choose from the wishes, affirmations, and auto-suggestions provided below, or write them yourself. You can also take help from my programme to write your wishes.

When You Lose Your Job

"There are no lost opportunities in the divine mind as one door is shut and another door is opened."

"I want a job of… (write specific job profile, designation) with gross earnings per annum Rs…or $… with… (write specific perks and benefits) before 2021-12-31. Now manifest it under the grace in a perfect way."

For Promotion and Hike in Salary

"I want to become.../or promoted to the rank of...with hike of $...or Rs...with benefits such as company car, etc. in my company before 2021-12-31, and want to share its fruits with my family and other needy people, now manifest it under the grace in a perfect way by my divine right, thank you."

Loss in Shares or Business

"I deny loss, there is no loss in divine mind therefore I can't lose my investments in shares/mutual funds/securities etc. and divine intelligence always guides me when to book profit or remain in it, which is best in my divine interest as I care and share with others and needy, thank you."

For Setting Financial Target in Life

"I want to earn...million $ or...Rupees by 2023/2028/2033 or by the time I retire at the age of... Or at the age of...and want to share the wealth with my family and others who are in need, now manifest it under the grace of God in a perfect way by my divine right."

For Growth of Business/Company

"I want that my business should grow and I reach a turnover of $...or Rupees...Lac/Cr per annum by 2023/2028/2033/2045 and want to share these earnings with employees, family, and the needy, now manifest it under the grace of God in a perfect way by my divine right, thank you."

For setting up New Business/Company

"I want to start a new business of...with a capital of $...or Rs...and I want all resources in terms of capital, infrastructure, finance, people, machinery, collaboration, government approvals/permissions, and to complete its operation within 2/3/4 years from now or by this...date and want to share its fruits with everyone in the company and those in need or to open hospital/educational institution/trust for the benefit of all those who need it for charitable cause, now manifest it under the grace of God in a perfect way by my divine right, thank you."

Marriage: Selection of life Partner

"The partner selected in heaven for me is brought in my life at once and I am married with my and everybody's satisfaction, now manifest it under the grace of God in a perfect way by my divine right before...(.date) thank you," (to be read by boy or girl).

"The partner selected in heaven for my daughter/son is brought in her/his life at once and she/he is married with her/his and everybody's satisfaction. Now manifest it under the grace of God in a perfect way by my divine right before this date…thank you." (To be read by parents or relatives or anyone else with some modifications.)

Illness

"There is no disease in the divine mind, therefore I can't have any disease."

"I want to recover completely from my present illness, keep myself fit for the benefit of my family, work, and to fulfil my goal of life, now manifest it under the grace of God in a perfect way by my divine right by this date… thank you."

"I have a healthy mind and body."

"I am healthy in mind, body, and spirits."

To Recover from Serious Illness

"I rest and relax in the love of God as God loves me and the power of God within me flows in my every organ of my mind and body, hence I am healed. Thank you."

"Divine love floods my consciousness with health and every cell in my mind and body is filled with light, I am now in perfect health. Thank you." (To be read by patient.)

To be read for the patient by his near and dear:

"My… (Father, mother, son, or daughter) rest and relax in the love of God as God loves him/her and the power of

God within him/her flows in his/her every organ of his/her mind and body, hence he/she is healed. Thank you."

Choose a Career

"Infinite spirit opens the way for my divine design of life to manifest, let me know what for I am for my best in my life, let it come before me now and I achieve it in a perfect way by the grace of God. Thank you."

"Infinite spirit opens the way for my immediate supply, let all that is mine by divine right now reach me in a great avalanche of abundance and give me a definite lead. Let me know if there is anything for me to do."

"Infinite spirit opens the way for my divine design of life to manifest, let the genius within me now be released. Let me see clearly the perfect plan."

"All doors are open for happy surprises and the divine plan of my life is speeded up under the grace."

"I now see clearly the perfect plan of my life; divine enthusiasm fires me and I fulfil my destiny."

For Demand of Money

Choose anyone of the following:

"Infinite intelligence opens the way for my immediate supply, my life is filled with prosperity, thank you."

"God is my unfailing supply and large sums of money come to me quickly under the grace in perfect ways."

"Infinite intelligence opens the heavens treasure to me and I am filled with unlimited, unfailing, and abundant supply, thank you."

"Infinite intelligence opens the way for my unlimited supply, and money, and wealth come to me easily, quickly, and effortlessly in perfect ways by my divine right, thank you."

"God is my unfailing and immediate supply."

"Money, peace, harmony, happiness, love, and success all come to me instantaneously and effortlessly."

"Infinite spirit I give thanks that the enormous sums of money which are mine by divine right reach me under the grace in perfect ways."

For delay in supply

"Declaring spirit was never too late and supply was at hand."

"There is time and space in divine mind therefore the word reaches instantly its destination and does not return void."

Ill will against anyone

Affirm and say repeatedly when you have ill will against anyone to clear your mind from negativity:

"I forgive and forget anyone who has ever offended me."

"I can control my temper."

"I am open and free."

When you start the day in morning

"Thy will be done this day, today is the day of completion, I give thanks for this perfect day. Miracle shall follow miracles and the wonders shall never cease."

"This is the day which God hath made; we will rejoice and be glad in it." × 2 times.

"O God within, give us heavenly kingdom which is pleasant to live in." × 3 times.

"O God give us heaven's unlimited supply on all levels." × 3 times.

General Prayers for Self

"I love everybody and everybody loves me, I am peaceful, happy, and satisfied. There is no effect of negative thoughts and negative suggestions on my divine mind and my life. I am healthy, powerful, and prosperous and I can achieve and get anything at once if I wish. Wealth comes to me by itself and I have plenty for me and to share. My life is the key to my success."

"Day by day in every way I am getting better and better."

"Peace is still; my mind is calm and receptive to the inspiration of God; He guides me and directs me." (Say repeatedly for few minutes.)

"Peace is still; I am heir to the wealth of God; I have plenty to use and to share." (Say repeatedly for few minutes.)

"Peace is still; my body is relaxed, I am renewed, strengthened and healed." (Say repeatedly for few minutes.) Note: The above three affirmations are taken from Theosophical Society of India, Annie Besant.

Say and affirm in the morning and night when you go to sleep:

"God is my help in every need,

God does my every hunger feed,

God walks beside me guides my way,

through every moment of the day.

I now am wise, I now am true,

Patient, kind, and loving too.

All things I am, can do, and be,

through God, the love and truth that is in me."

For Solution to Problems

"O Divine, order now."

"We are identified in love with the spirit of everyone connected with… (company, person, thing, let the divine ideas come out of this situation and we receive the right amount/solution/justice/judgement/share by my divine right. Thank you."

"I cast my burden on God within and I go free."

"I cast my burden of luck on God within and I go free to have plenty."

Protection and to Clear Mind from All Fears

"I am safe and protected."

"Negative thoughts and negative suggestions have no influence over me on any level of my mind."

"I love everybody and everybody loves me, I am safe and protected."

"There is no fear in divine mind so I am free and protected."

"I am surrounded by the white light of "Jesus/Krishna/Rama/Allah/Waheguru, nothing can penetrate Him and I am safe and protected."

"When God is there, I have nothing to fear."

"I am free of all negative karma. I live in the law of grace and start anew with a clean slate."

"I am now fearless, courageous, and bold."

Reducing Weight and Becoming Slim

"I am slim and trim."

"I can lose weight; I am attracted to good and nourished stuff."

Stop Smoking

"I am stronger by will and can stop smoking."

"I breathe clean, fresh air; I am stronger than any bad habit. I am happy to quit smoking."

To Find a Lost Thing

"There is no loss in divine mind, therefore I can't lose my… (mention the lost item), I will either get it back or will get its equivalent."

Spiritual Enhancement

"May Lord of light and bliss, grant us prosperity. May the guiding spirit of the firmament and Goddess of riches, grant us prosperity. May the adorable and resplendent Lord prop us. O spirit of invincible fullness, thou bestow all prosperity upon us. Full of sweetness are the plants and full of sweetness are my words, and with the things that are full of sweetness, I prosper in thousand ways."

"With Earth as a lamp, with swelling sea as the ghee and with the hot-rayed Sun as the flame, I have seen the Lord and laid at the feet of the red-flaming discus, this garland of words so that my sea of troubles may vanish."

"O Thou who art at home, deep in my heart, enables me to join you deep in my heart."

"O how amicable are thy dwellings Lord of hearts. My soul has a desire and longing to enter the courts of the Lord, my heart and my flesh rejoice in the living God."

"I am open and free; I love and appreciate myself exactly as I am, and love everybody as they are."

"I look forward to increase my spirituality and understanding as I set forth on this journey."

"I take charge of my life and trust my inner being to lead me in the right path."

"I confess all my sins, please erase all my sins from my subconscious mind and I am connected to the divine."

"I am a radiant being filled with light and love."

"I am opening my heart with love all around me."

"I am tuned with the Universe/God/Jesus/Rama/Allah/Waheguru/infinite spirit/intelligence."

"I have all the energy I need."

"I am full of love; I radiate love and happiness all around me."

Loan Approval

"I am identified in love with the spirit of everyone connected with the bank… (Name of bank or financial institution). Let the divine ideas come out of this situation and I receive my loan approval of $…or Rs…"

Suggestions for Corporate/Business Houses to Increase Turnover and Expand Business

The companies and business people who do not care for their customers/clients/employees go in losses, closures, lockouts, and some mishaps in their companies/business because they ignore the natural law of sharing with others. Such companies never go for charity which is why they don't grow much. The companies who care and share with all and do some percentage of profits as charities annually or make trusts are definite to grow as big groups.

The board meeting are the deciding factors for the future fate of the companies as they speak, write, publish, and announce for shareholders, employees, and discuss present and future strategies to target business and growth.

Every company can grow if their management is fair in dealing and sharing with all in positive way and such companies visualize the growth as to what will be their turnover down the line in 1 to 3/5 years from the present. They can grow further if they have multi-level action on ground as per the laws of sharing, big thoughts, fairness, and command to work and take risks. If the management has no goals for the futures and happy to continue with the present, then they cannot grow in the future as they are responsible to create their destiny for their own companies.

The corporate houses/businessman can also use this programme separately to increase the turnover and growth for their companies/businesses.

To Grow Company or Business

You should do this programme and make a wish and follow the same procedure, write wish slip as given below;

"I want from my God within to provide me all the tools, resources, finances, people, collaboration, plans, machinery, approvals, networking, customer base, technology, services for increasing my turnover from present...$billion to double within 1/2/3 years from now by this date...This is what I want God within and want to share some percentage of profits with my shareholders, partners, for charitable cause, and employees. Now manifest it under the grace of God in a perfect way. Thank you."

My complete and perfect wish

"In divine mind there is only completion, therefore I complete my wish with my perfect work, my sufficient wealth, my perfect home, and my perfect health under the grace in a perfect way. I am thankful."

Generate big thoughts and create them

"I am standing tall, I am thinking tall, and I believe tall."

"Whenever I set a definite goal, I take quick action towards its attainment to create and sustain massive momentum."

"My greatest good is aiming to me now and is manifesting in my life right now."

"I respect my desires, intensions, and dreams and take great satisfaction in making daily progress."

"I plan each day and I follow my plan; I review my plan every morning."

"I deserve the best and it comes to me right now."

"I constantly keep my desires and plans in my mind at all times and I am now on my way to success."

"Life is easy and I have abundance for what I need."

"I am free of the past and the future; the moment I live in is now, with no history affecting my choices in the present."

"I reach the fullest potential in my life and always aim and apply with great success."

"I am enjoying my life and I am doing exactly what I should be doing at this time."

"Everyone is God sent to teach me; teacher is everywhere and life is my guru (teacher)."

'I am in complete control of my mind; I now have the ability to think the way I choose."

To Free Yourself from Debt/Mortgage

"There is no debt/mortgage in divine mind, all is squared. All my obligations are wiped out under the grace in perfect ways. Thank you."

Terms and Conditions

"This agreement is between the owners of the programme, "Enlighten the Lamp of your Fortune" in legal term "Mentor" and the person who is doing this programme is called "Programmer." It is construed that the programmer has read the book and all the terms and conditions and by reading it, has agreed to these terms and conditions detailed below, and by accepting has agreed to follow all of our terms and conditions".

1. This programme is of spiritual and mental nature, it's success will solely depend on the God's will and His manifestation, and how committed you are to do this programme, so the Mentor shall not be responsible personally or legally for the results obtained through this programme and is not binding on "the author" in any way.

2. Mentor cannot guarantee the program's success which will depend on the programmer's mindset and God's will.

3. The programme, "Enlighten the Lamp of your Fortune" is for good causes/charities and part of the earnings and collection will go for charitable causes, this needs to be noted. Hence the money paid shall not be refunded in any circumstance.

4. Any legal suits in any circumstance shall have to be in the jurisdiction of Kanpur City, UP, India, only.

5. The creation is a part of mind and God's grace, so the success of the programme will depend on the will of God and not me (Mentor), the owner of the programme and I am only the mentor in this programme. The programme is indicative only for making dreams possible which will depend on individual factors as described here in the terms and conditions and the website pages. The programmer has read all the pages before he/she goes for this programme is construed and accepted the credibility of the programme.

6. In case of any bad event, loss, or harm in physical, financial, personal, and mental form and in any eventuality is the responsibility of the person who is doing the programme (the programmer) and not the mentor, the owner of the programme in any way.

7. No compensation is paid to anyone (the programmer) who is doing this programme if anyone bears any

loss, harm, or any event which is not in the interest of the programmer and they are not binding on the mentor, to pay anyone as this is the sole responsibility of the programmer who is doing the programme.

8. The programmer is solely responsible for the events related after or during the programme. The role of the mentor is only to help and show direction and not the ultimate results which is the responsibility of the programmer and his personal performance and other factors like God's will, positivity, trust etc., given here in the terms.

9. The programmer will ensure that this programme is done for only good causes for his/her dreams manifestations, prosperity, solution to problems, and in no way the programmer may try to harm any person or persons through this programme. It is strictly not allowed and the programmer agrees not to do this programme to harm anyone.

10. This programme is solely for the mentor who is doing this programme and the mentor agrees not to pass the content of the programme and the content of website to any other person/persons and shall not copy or reproduce it in any other format which is strictly not allowed. In case if the mentor at any stage reproduces or copies the programme and markets or sells the programme, he/she is liable to legal suit and compensation from the mentor.

11. The programmer will be informed to interact with the mentor during the course of programme if any such request comes from the mentor will depend on the queue and the on chat, emails, video conference, telephone etc., hence programmer will have to wait for his/her turn and shall be informed accordingly.

12. Programmer will have to maintain cordial relationship with mentor and should obey the instructions as per programme for making it a success and any deviation from this such as misbehaving, use of bad language, and disobeying the instructions of mentor and as given in the programme content, mentor has the right to discard the programmer and stop helping the mentor through emails, chats, video conference, telephone, and personal interviews as per the plan which is selected by the programmer. It is a relationship of a teacher/mentor with a student or a guru with disciple which the programmer should understand and shall have to agree.

13. Mentor has every right to change, add, or delete anything in the content of the website and the programme at any point of time and shall not liable to inform the programmer. Mentor is also not liable to reply to the programmer in event of such changes if any, and programmer should follow the instructions in the content and accept in special cases where the mentor thinks it is necessary to convey the programmer which is the prerogative of the mentor.

14. The programmer shall have to maintain strict secrecy while doing the programme to make it a success and should not discuss or reveal it to other persons, by revealing and discussing it with others may jeopardize the programme and appropriate results cannot be achieved.

15. Wish fulfilment will depend on the patience of the programmer so he/she has to wait for the time for the success of the programme. Programmer should maintain it and should agree to this clause.

16. The programmer has to undertake all actions required on ground to facilitate the programme's success and merely by doing this programme makes no sense in achieving the results hence the programmer has to make all actions required in the direction of wish, dream, goal, and solution to individual problems.

Dinesh Sahay
Author
Owner of the programme
Enlighten the Lamp of your Fortune/Make Your Dreams Come True
ds.makeyourdreams@gmail.com
quey.makeyourdreams@gmail.com